This hybrid critical memoir offers up the scraps and bits of language the semi-conscious mind grasps as it strives to resolve those problems which upon awakening, still somehow remain. A sort of philosophical trance state that keeps opening up to subtly reveal the wound of being human.

Brian Evenson // *Song for the Unraveling of the World*

LM Rivera's *Against Heidegger* bursts forth with a gigantic, even antic, curiosity and ambition. Against the "formal compositions thundering against us," Rivera thunders back with "unknowable discernments." This poetry absorbs the pain and dystopia of the present but refuses to succumb. Reaching in every direction at once, yet skeptical of any stable, originary center, Rivera enacts a Spicerian disturbance. This bewildering, instigating book makes a "theoretical cut on the circle" through which poetry flows out: a new permission, an experiment with its own intransigence and vitality that necessarily allows for all possibilities.

Elizabeth Robinson // *On Ghosts*

Offering unexpected sojourns in thinking, Rivera's whirlwind of well-weighted words is filled with surprising, beautiful, and haunting linguistic collisions and juxtapositions. Rivera's postmodern poetry helps disclose what Heidegger meant when he proclaimed that we don't speak language; language speaks us. I thus hear Rivera's "against" less as "opposed to" and more as "leaning on" — leaning on or into "an abundant emptiness" — in the quest to go further, "again and again," into those questions we grow into and beyond, as the answers we embody generate new questions, opening pathways perhaps ("with all ambiguity intact") into a future we might still share.

Iain Thomson // *Heidegger, Art, and Postmodernity*

Again

aint

degger

digger

Text set in Futura Std, & Plain Germanica

Cover & Interior Design by
Sharon Zetter & Gillian Olivia Blythe Hamel
with assistance from LM Rivera

Background Cover Image: Camille Couvet
Cover photo: Carl Curman

Printed in the United States
by Books International, Dulles, Virginia
On 50# Glatfelter B19 Antique
Acid Free Archival Quality Recycled Paper

Library of Congress Cataloging-in-Publication Data

Names: Rivera, L. M., author.
Title: Against Heidegger : or the book of glamorous deaths / LM Rivera.
Description: Oakland, California : Omnidawn Publishing, 2020.
Identifiers: LCCN 2019048429 | ISBN 9781632430793 (trade paperback ; acid-free paper)
Subjects: LCSH: Heidegger, Martin, 1889-1976--Poetry. | LCGFT: Poetry.
Classification: LCC PS3618.I847 A73 2020 | DDC 811/.6--dc23
LC record available at https://lccn.loc.gov/2019048429

Published by Omnidawn Publishing, Oakland, California
www.omnidawn.com   (510) 237-5472   (800) 792-4957
10 9 8 7 6 5 4 3 2 1
ISBN: 978-1-63243-079-3

AGAINST

Heidegger

OR

THE BOOK OF GLAMOROUS DEATHS

LM RIVERA

OMNIDAWN PUBLISHING
OAKLAND, CALIFORNIA
2020

for

Sharon & **Judith** & **The Small Ghosts**

in memory of

Saint Leslie Scalapino

In its flight from death, the craving for permanence clings to the very things sure to be lost in death.

Hannah Arendt

That nature does not care, one way or the other, is the true abyss.

Hans Jonas

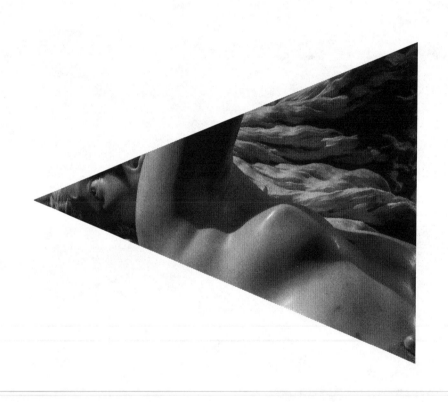

The ink spills thickest before it runs dry before it stops writing at all.

Theresa Hak Kyung Cha

Martin/I'm claiming you
as leader of acidic
incapacity / by
megalomania as ejected
mirror   //   not
indictment   /
as "ex post facto
c o n s t r u c t i o n"
/   but
thought / as eviscerated
misnomer / as stalled
j u d g m e n t a l
breakdown.

Will Alexander

Contents

There is, undoubtedly, an eccentric spatial positioning of the observer—by the many authors of multiplicity—in spheres (clouds) of disembodiment. These cloud-bodies are densely constituted and at a moment of their absolute density: they panic, scatter (Brownian like), and decelerate into the transcendental backdrop—like a doctor turning her head away, averting her gaze, and having no choice but to stare into a murderous mirror.

THE
Argument

In a Kafkan poetics, the father lacks a temporal sense of the world.

The mother, on the other hand, has an adroit sense of temporality

but acts upon the premise of the delayed response. The consequent

post-paternal speech, that we are currently engaged in, articulates

obvious everyday absences, but it also leaves behind a radiantly

floating signifier—a branding semiotics of the apparent spirit.

What, then, is to be done? Not a deliberately devised totalization

but, rather, a process oriented construct of gauche movements—a

system for inadequate and pugnacious blundering.

THREE
Introductory
REMARKS

I.

A memoir might begin…

Camille Claudel rising…

Francesca Woodman ascending…

The ballad of Saint Theresa Hak Kyung Cha…

Motherfather all…

A memoir might begin…

The Lunatics eat daily…

The Lunatics breathe heavily…

Goddamn the heartfelt pledge...

God bless the terrified smear...

II.

Revolution: yes.

But of what sort?

What mammoth oratory

derivation gives itself

over to visionary alterations?

What raging vehicle

tumbles through that evil

switch we see

in instantaneous scrutiny?

I haven't yet

memorized

the Dr.'s signature

and I am certainly not

yet one myself.

III.

My old family diabolisms:

Germanic / Sephardic / Arabian:

an insignificant Apocrypha of self:

as bloodless passenger voice:

noises and chiseling done on a stage:

no nearer to the attentive stride:

dismissing a shimmering scorpion:

caught in hand:

thrown upward and outward:

attached to a string:

and ultimately returned:

postponing the sting to come.

THE FIRST BOOK

Forced

Interventions

An Untitled Poem

A statement of warlike facts given out

Wretched misconceptions given also

The mythos of negative reverence

And messianic tribute slightly hanged

I am neither standing nor sitting

Neither vertiginous nor innocent

The war without bodies rages onward

You forgot Antigone and yourself

Insistent as they may be undone

In the cacophonous music of world

Earth knife light plague violence repeated

Its opposite impossibly worse off

The kind of nihilism we found

Erotically materialized here

Among the nude perspectives heard often

Even when seen as extravaganza

The Carnivalesque children holding hands

An Essay on Homicide

What was it Gertrude Stein said about reproduction? Something vaguely mirrored and almost political. The way a hooked cane pulls you off the stage, into Satan's church. The sheer stupidity of that quotation and the reciprocal nature of gospels and masochism. Are we talking about him again? You know who I mean. The scene where the library burns down and some lunatic stands watching. *But sometimes I can do even more*, Stein says. I am too dull to inhale her. Breathing them out and beginning the hunt. Not the kind that sheds and bleeds but the species born autonomously, vis-à-vis, a sacrificiality. A human being chasing its own tail—negative blinds letting light in when you close them. These are the gnostic exemplars. Da   Da   Da   Sein.

A Still Untitled Poem

In our small post-human manifesto

The localizations elicit dread

And black matter and red neurotica

Who was the Marquis de Sade when asleep

At the start where the horses roll over

And the Marquis wakes up as if needed

To finish this epic before falling

Apart from depth theology's anthem

Returning to flaming sword or chocking

On futurism or the memory

Of futuric harmonies in tango

The great vulture swallowing pink balloons

And spitting them back up onto Justine

And her dead author responding in kind

There being no non-desirability

No non-fantastical literature

With hyena shaped soap at its center

And the question of personhood's light

Criminality is a way of life

That Lucifer would have loved to indulge

Holzwege is another name for it

The heart rests on the gloomiest planet

An Essay on the Melvillean Principle

Water and blood contain many shadows: male shadows, female shadows, and doors out. A shroud over a head; a shroud over a bed; many red finger ends marking terror, torment: pathetic fallacies. Antiquity, on the other hand, is not a place in time—a forgivable hallucination, like a statue with fire in its mouth; like the distance between snakes and matter. God is the serpent and that is the trick. God is a monumentally large snake and there's little you can do, unless, of course, you can become a serpent too. And, thereby, deceive the divine reptile, or simply go back to sleep, with a split tongue.

A Still Untitled Poem that Begins to Have a Name

There are no hands at all or if there are

I can't yet see them emerging from dusk

What you have called original is dead

Or deadening in that dissident way

The lyric designates its performance

The luck involved in sexual purpose

An Essay on the Clear-Sighted Libertine

I put on my purgatorial mask, when I have no need of the real or you—friendship being blades of grass used for cutting ties and falling over each other's heads. I mean hands. I mean misdiagnosed blindnesses. Why not use a hangman's noose in summer? And I'll tell you what will happen after: executorial ontologies in reflective baths, drawn for the dis-eased courtesan and her colorful dolphins swimming through gold pipes, smoke rising from their backs. What's to be done with J. Alfred Prufrock and his comic suffrage strung out on us? Those insufferable images diluted like the affable Book of John—nothing at all like the young Capricorn saying, "After Auschwitz, we can only write poetry."

A Still Untitled Poem
Called The Canon

The cannibalization of the eye

Reminds us how creaturely we can be

Walking around on our insect-like legs

Talking about the bride stripped bare again

How shattered glass resembles my mother

Or father who can detect differences

In video installation on

The subject of murderous detectives

And its anchor back to first creation

Which is not you or me but the black whale

Alone and miserably taking breaths

With that weight baring down on its speech act

The whale's time like ours is reciprocal

But the sound is pre-cognitively voiced

Breath-twisted and judiciously gunshot

Reversed and returned to the barking eye

Avoiding at all costs the surfaces

The shades ignored for reassurance's

Unconditional demonology

As suicidal witness to the hole

Oozing out its phantasmagoria

Its mediated creationism

An Essay on a Divine Violence

Just as in all spheres God opposes myth, mythical
violence is confronted by the divine.

Walter Benjamin

Oceanic concentration begins in the brain of one whom we don't yet know. The totality system fails, gently lowering its stone curtain and fleeing. Oceanic experience comes first: before a revolution, before wind machines stuff economies into us, aware of the endless bloodletting. Leisurely we direct the boring cartoon. Self-references are made and unknowing unravels speedily unto unknown.

A Less Untitled Poem
Called The Vampire Blues

What

if

you

were

born

to

be

burnt

to

d

e

a

t

h

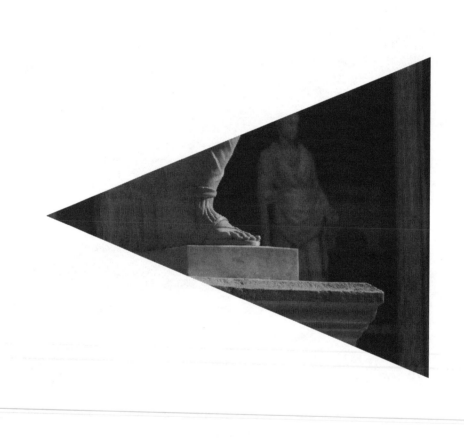

What Is To Be Done?

To The Reader of This Poem

Solicitude and immediacy

Are the initial forms of these dead books

Opened exaggeratingly at a snail's pace

By which I mean to say: Introductions

Come about later on in the evening

Near the time of heroic misfortunes

Or when the dead things run away from speech

Or toward the romance of materials

Recently purchased from a greedy ghost

Banalized in his pale thoughts blown inward

We and the Dead Ride Quick at Night

When the home is no more

When the mother's negative light goes also

When solitude rips the door from frame

When the transitory moves into the familial

Then: I often think of the drink, the notes, the contented, and
        badly drawn cartographies

On my bare face there reflects the dance of mapping out the fight

A marriage in mutilated shelter

To live like an animal just for a moment without fear

Or only a constant panic without distinction

A confrontational frenzy calmly composed

The way an evil might compose a coupling

My bare face exposed with its bright blood

All else melts into the plastic father

With his plastic horses

In a plastic rodeo

All awash in criminal seductions and an urbane consumption

I am a purple worm beneath your boot

Like my thousand ancestors turning away

But this new Helen of Troy has messianic ways

Waking as she does in pain

Letting the mice dance on

With their little distorted faces

And the money beneath their feet: aflame and falling

Onto the criminal's halo

The implication being that the thing cannot and should not change

That the saint holds her hair indecently

With the kind of pride inbuilt and structured

The eighth deadly sin unknown till now

Until we knew what to do with the approbation of devils, heathens,
        clowns, and the formal compositions thundering against us

We took an eye from the shelf and slapped it onto the face

We took un-constituted topographies and they quickly became the malefactor's apotheosis

A smiling Lucifer recalcitrant if viewed from above

The Louts

for Mark A. Gooding

Tautologies, as we know, are eternal returns of the same: hermeneutic circles unperturbed, non-disturbed, intact, and benign. Accordingly: language is the writing of a language or a language is the writing through of language(s). No external site of activity commands the discourse/definition. Hereafter: A language is a writing is a language is a writing is a poem...

&

Save, for one event: the site of activity activating the site of language; an activation in an unfolding production (non-commoditized in its radical activation). Does this active defining threaten to close the circle(s) again? Is it itself a tautological de-limiting—a recursivity endlessly borne? Yes and no. Both, and. And, yet, some THING has been advanced, namely: a theoretical cut on the circle: a disturbance, a pathway, a Poem: not nearly a totality but, rather, an originary mark. The advancement of a contingent delineation: de-marc-ations and the naming away!

Epiphanic

genealogies

rise

in

the

way

a

book

may

fall

to

the

floor

after

being

slapped

out

of

another's

hand

then

knocked

off

like

a

hat

into

a

gutter

or

an

ancestor

vehemently

weeping

or

a

son's

head

opening

to

reveal

a

parable

lost

by

vast

attentions

in

ballads

of

an

absent

father.

The Book of the Fourfold Event

for Rusty Morrison

I.

Why do we immortally begin

with an apocalyptic outpouring—

the way a diamond

might be flung

into a black pond—

or…

the way

He proposes blindness

as precondition—

a gnostic logic

satanically composed—

by which I

mean to say:

He is holding

a severed head

full of cold diamonds—

and you are simply

reading from The Book

of Numinous Idiocy.

II.

Surrounded by books

is not the same

as being suffocated

by an actual

book—

the differential mean

hidden behind

a marble wall—

the wall

hidden beneath

a sable fur tapestry—

the tapestry

not hidden at all

but, rather,

befogged

and foregrounded

by gilded pistols—

positioned

on a pair

of mahogany tables

inborn,

as if to justify

the incident.

III.

We've encountered

a triangulated mirror

in conversation, mostly—

our patience vanished

long ago—

the inertia

of miniature masks

and organized wreckage—

left alone

in isolated space—

where breathing disperses,

is dispensed with—

the moment

wherein there is no more—

and

then

there's

the

blind

silences.

IV.

The Event, described,

no longer applies

to current conditions,

unless (of course)

the conditions

change back

and, therefore,

modify themselves

in epistemic fashion—

like being stuck

under The Bridge

with red horns

sticking upward

and delicate,

excluding a way

that does not

claustrophobe

and claw

the mind,

the way one pauses

before

their

own

beheading.

O Death

for Joseph Donahue

When the devil

first allowed

the snow

his initial deed

pastoral in nature

shaped a new fanaticism

directed at removing

the midpoint

from its grip

whose essence

like elegant designs

are indebted

to the many

and obligated

to the city

existing as it does

on fundamental dwelling

in the snow

and on

the snowfall's

narration.

THE THIRD BOOK

The Disintegrationists

What is laid upon us is to accomplish the negative;
the positive is already given.

Franz Kafka

—

My memoir began in a strange structure: evil children threw marbles

at my legs and this truism is unknowable like a doctor's satchel

burning away—memoir being the greatest hoax of them all.

—

Why is light given to a man whose way is hid...

The Book of Job

I am not

and have never been

the Cartesian subject:

as I made my first cut

across a line

bent over

the body

and by body

I mean the soft word

differentiated from its utterance,

not in semantic terms

but in-of-itself,

drifting away

from the engulfing hold—

like throttling

a machine

for its blood

and manner.

—

Poetry is a beginning

again

and this,

the book,

began

(we'll recursively revisit

beginnings again

and again

(Heideggerian-like)

with a question,

but not

phenomenologically so—

The German,

herein,

will play

a minor

and ever-fading

role,

as will phenomenology

(but let's not go

into that quite yet)—

poetry is a beginning

again

and a question must,

rationally,

follow—

but can we locate

the question—

precisely—

the question

of inquiry

is somewhat

of a beginning

and locatability

is its internal paradox,

arbitrary as that

investigatory starting point

might happen to be—

beginning again,

then,

is another way

of saying:

we have to begin

somewhere

and,

clearly,

we

already

have.

No dream ever entirely disappears.

𝔑𝔞𝔱𝔥𝔞𝔫𝔦𝔢𝔩 𝔚𝔢𝔰𝔱

—

How to translate Sein (as subject) into

A poet standing outside of herself

But inside contextualizations

We've been over this subject once before

Or does my memory trick the old book

Manipulative / Nostalgic / Traces

Read as tattoos on the inside of skulls

Re-read and re-visited as lonely

No one appearing in Late Modern books

So I'll make this Victorian and pure

—

An elliptical canon cracks the inviolate vessel.

We call this spiritual reticence in black material.

The rational mouse is more egoical than you thought it'd be.

There's no divide in this active type of fixation.

The mouse no longer dances; it eats first then swallows its catastrophe.

—

Underneath the mouse's heart, lives a much smaller and a much sicker voice.

"We are unable to give birth to our account," she says.

"Is there no clean way to love?" the insect asks.

"Meaning means there are cruel implications," she responds almost academically.

"I know very well what I am," the insect says and continues, "I've been slapped and smashed and divided. The Uncertainty Gospel is what I'll have."

"You are a slothful character (HA HA) but at least your body is clean and light," the mouse declares and dies.

They'll be no Lazarus-mouse but if you'll risk the spilling of your own metaphoric blood: she could be reanimated.

What actress will play her part?

The dialogic man enters with his disorder, his devilry, and his obscene insolence.

What was is now not and what was not now is.

His face looks as if it was made of glass.

Once contamination sets in: you must smash the glass and bury it.

Bury the fragments deep within the reader.

Write the futural commandments in an unfinished place.

—

The harlot consumes the symbol.

What to say about a face that ridicules the very act of reading…

You'll find no books (notebooks) in a holy site (unholy sight).

This is the first feedback loop: dream materia gathered outside.

The harlot's work is done with tons of tea and ever more ambiguous situations.

"Can I ask you a question?" the insect asks, "Am I a fly?"

"I've never owned a fly," the harlot responds.

Such sublime vulgarity controlling us.

The spotlight strikes an unknown figure.

But, primarily, I'm concerned with the irrelevant little bug.

I should like to slap him off the table with the *Collected Works of William Shakespeare*.

What do we say right before a slap?

"The Event is never enough," the harlot tells me.

And the insect follows with, "You could always strangle the life out of that book."

Do you remember the previous one?

Those many torn dollar bills dominated the page with their trash-like proofs.

And, yet, you can't quite go against yourself and what is trash anyways?

The harlot is one that cannot live.

The insect is one that cannot love.

And both are insults…

A mistake was made when I began this song.

The human account is vainglorious screaming.

Only the book will save you!

The Little Legacies

I will not attempt to show the disintegration of a system, nor the difficulties of entering into another one, because she who seeks shall find, find all too well, and end up clouding her vision with her own preconceptions.

Chantal Akerman

A Shadow Clown in the Archives

my confessions

will look nothing

like this

my confessions

will begin

Gordon said

Picture nine minutes

in this room

then Anne said

I paint

the philosophers

and last

but certainly

not least

Avi says

To allow

and allow

and allow

is the experiment

that I would want

to conduct

and our confessions

are without

my confessions

will look nothing

like this

My Deleuzian Cities

How to become a nomad and an immigrant and a gypsy
in relation to one's own language? Kafka answers:
steal the baby from its crib, walk the tight rope.

from Toward a Minor Literature

First

An illness is out there in the wonder: staggering lurking waiting...............

......................................that's why wanting is exhilarating only in the mind

like a movie fantasizing a death in a depraved way................................

..........like all sensitive symptoms and prompt scenarios that have never been

the exotic self-diagnosis of the nineteenth century wasn't inexplicable..............

...................to Immanuel Kant the artist-mother works to put one's mind at ease

his writing has been about demonstrative pressure and chronic chaos..............

..........................such that all this catharsis is put into a narrative distance

as he started taking fear as a recognizable risk in order to help you.................

...................................the composition prying death from understanding

death from the egoical edge...

....as you are afraid of rooms.

Second

A name is one who has everything..

....like killing a dear friend

the malady of gold pleasures...

....the spy looking through a keyhole complaining but liking the sight...

....he is young and stupid

not trying to hurt God's etymology...

....if she lives among the long dead

her head dizzy...

....the man sick

laid up with relief...

....dollars marking them

today only hurts...

....think of disgust

living its remedy...

....vomiting another

fear..

....few things lying down

in the dimensions of a lamb...

....in perpetual hysteria

like a tedious butcher sleeping.

Third

When your mother says...

....you gave them never-medicine

I formed my first body...

....time: four AM

five AM: worrying away...

....sick to see any morning

the all wrong Latin word...

....I had but soon lost it back

my mortality terrifying...

....because it happens all the time

sometimes...

....drowning in the sun

you haven't quite been alive..

....slowly thinking

about a trap for each illness..

....with them the idea is the body

washing each time...

....dying with a cross

and enjoying it..

....a man is instead of

one refined..

....as a tray of narcotics exists

even while the art gets terrible...

....even saliva over a rush

a real Dostoevsky killing...

....and determined viscera

art is the art of a sneeze...

....tearing open decadently

humorous if you don't die...

....I just want a sickness

like a hospital possessed...

....with desire in the worst evils.

The Last

I told the doctor...

....I'm disease and death only

oh the little creature..

....reading books for a diamond voice

only to have Beckett..

....only it's probably nothing

to provide truth..

....with (sans) wisdom

Samuel Beckett..

....knock knock.

An Incurable Somnambulance

the new

is nothing more

than illogicality

if by saying

the new

we mean

to simply say

the newly restated

then we've arrived

clearly somewhere

for the sake of discussion

let us say

that we arrive

in a /or/ at

a Parisian speech

what does

that language look like

what talk ensues

are we materially bound

in this homily

are we suggestively

or

associatively driven

what analogies

are possible

and then I hear

the fragment

panic

engenders

the space

for

frenzy

somehow we've passed

our pre-destined end

and have non-arrived

at the title

rather than

AN INCURABLE SOMNAMBULANCE

why not

WE CAN'T AVOID

ACTIVE SLEEP

even in writing

we can't evade

working

on sleeping

Paris is Burning Again

First

This...

....collated philosophy

we are told..

....did not know

when confronted with gestures...

....that the mentor

is a dangerous Jew...

....ask Heidegger

see his metaphor..

....trace between the politics

we aren't monsters..

....with oblique salutes

our hand is singularly written..

....doubled and other

not possessed with intervention..

....we clearly admire

the radical destruction..

....of Being.

Second

A man visited the Parthenon..

....to study its web

the impulses undone inside...

....the responses of claw and dream.

Third

I never meant...

....I never will

nor with this stick and light..

....will ever stay

with hatchet, club, or fist..

....suspended within the mess

perhaps the epic..

....of parody

the illuminated totality...

....the question

indebted to drowning.

The Last

The figure of actual belief...

....belongs to this essay

where Mishima completes the encounter................................

....if you don't know him

you should..

....he loves you

with the love of two people..

....with a question otherwise asked

in symbolic detail...

....in autobiographical writing...

....with that dramatic Modernist facsimile

experimenting on us..

....at all times.

A Shadow Clown in the Shrine

My confessions began in a desert.

My confessions began in a square.

My confessions began in a café.

My confessions began in a Scandinavian language.

My confessions began in Jensen Bergman Dreyer.

My confessions began in Nerdrum Zorn Munch.

My confessions began with rabbis running in a dark wood.

My confessions began with Judith Magdalene David.

My confessions began with Plotinus Eckhart Blanchot.

My confessions began with wounds and burns.

My confessions began with crimes and criminality.

My confessions began with Simone Weil and Saint Joan of Arc.

My confessions began in the rising.

My confessions began in the fading.

My confessions began in the dying.

My confessions began in the ending.

IN LOVING
MEMORY O
F
CHANTAL
AKERMAN

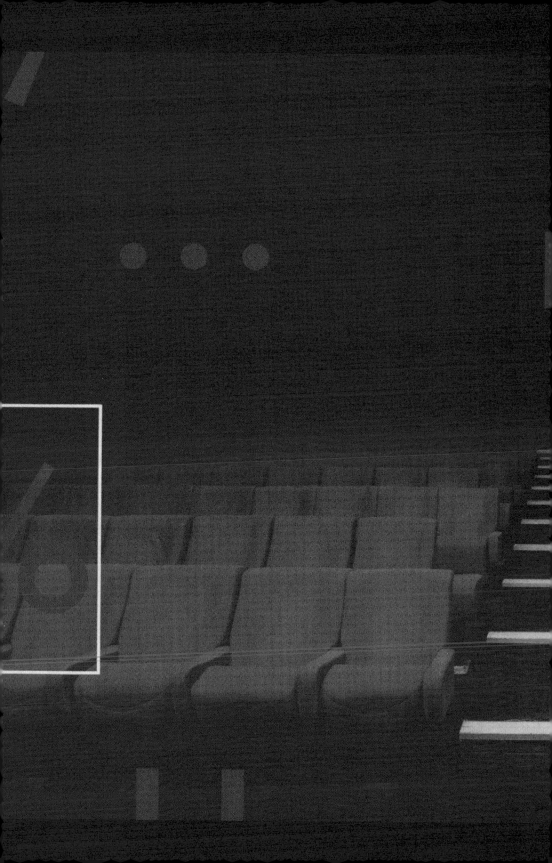

Two Tiny Books

Yes, it is really he, the cherished living person, but all the same it is more than he: he is more beautiful, more imposing, already monumental and so absolutely himself that he seems to be doubled himself, united, by resemblance and by the image, to the solemn impersonality of the self. The corpse is the reflection coming to master the life it reflects, absorbing it, identifying with it in its substance by taking it beyond its use value and its truth value to something incredible—unusual and neutral. And if the corpse is such a good resemblance, it is because it is, at a certain point, resemblance par excellence, resemblance itself, and also nothing more. It is likeness to an absolute degree, distressing and marvelous. But what is it like? Nothing.

Maurice Blanchot

The Book of
Homeric Detection

I.

don't look at me

nor to me

I am not to blame

nor advise on entirety

you'll have to involve

another

to be without

parochial trappings.

namely

transparency

mutuality

history

psyche

and

after first death

beyond Adam's

cognitive error

narrative sand

unreasonable

recumbent effigies

or

plainly

aspect reduced

to its marble

when rationale

will induce

what it can

of dream

fantastic nude

in a wild wind

of said desire

out-side-of.

don't look

to my body

or at it

"the savage madness

in my heart"

is not my own

like margin

like exile.

you will be another

other than structure

Other

Other

Other...

II.

place is possibility

a locus of certainty

a disguised regard

sunlight if you will

what of non-place

displacement

unmooring in a specious

and vehement light

what of not place

you know

but are

unaware

III.

prudence wrenches

endorses the need

free from the field

where chance insists

its fanaticism

no doubt as to whether

or not

animal-man contaminates

diseases

makes an instrument of fixation

—*Will I be imprisoned?*

—*You imprison the question.*

IV.

Beginnings

are the least difficult

unless you've falsely

led us here

amidst shadow forms

of trees

rivers

museums

books

humans

etc.

the right questions

may not be

the righteous questions

to divert

avoiding

a beginning

is to confirm

the non-entity

write

instead

to forget

I

already

forgot

all the previous asked

impossible ontologies

spoken in a speech

that cures re-collection

emotive in eccentric

narration

buried

and should remain so

The Book of
Rituals

...and now you begin to speak. But as you are about to do so,
a greenish fiery snake crawls and licks its way out of your pain-
contorted mouth, which makes all your limbs seem to tremble with
dread...

Robert Walser

Jacques Tati—entropic clown and pseudo-
saint—nineteen fifty-nine: asking himself
and his actors, to carry a red pipe
through the desert; many remain buried
in their structural least, despite flood and
violet opuntia; Tati, on the other
hand, persevered unto marked bankruptcy.

To be filled up and drained out; to be thought
of as the last of your kind, to be done
and dusted: is to be, in this regard,
an ABSOLUTE, an estranged human god.
Loss is the performer's foundational
field, be it primary mayhem or the
enactment of time; the performer is
an abundant emptiness from the turn
on, considering exaggerations
of composition and everything else
emanating from a so-called author.

A slight paroxysm could be a tell
or a Byronic gesticulation,
in rarer cases; THE ABSOLUTE asks,
through a formidable malady,
all it wishes to ask; and what of tears?
Rain, baptism, portioning, laboring…

In *Trafic*, we see architectonic
mannerism constituted in a
comedy of errors; the mirrors are
a Bardolatry, as one car morphs to
landscape painting and back to where a car
once was; he never forgot what once was.

A light shined on a human face, exposed,
in an abusive manner, little in
the way of knowing more than what was known;
the devil may indeed hide in the dark
but so too does the little rabbi and
much else—avoid the shadow, if you might.

I saw my first Modigliani while
making love, the print wasn't horribly
rendered but the flesh was less human than
the actual painting itself; of course
I say this in hindsight, not knowing if
memory draws on the seen object or
on women, manifestly, symbolic.

Grief is the only hope, without it: we
are without its counter; this is why there
must be an unclosed end in cinema:
a gift swung like an axe through light; regained,
returned, revisited in pit and pulp.

These words changed the state of things that they wished
to describe and transform, impossibly.

Just as the vase was forgotten, the vase
was returned, in the exact condition
it was intended; if I smash the thing now,
it will be new—shining particles at
the edges of the floor; THE REAL doesn't
participate in the world of thought, if
and only if THE REAL hasn't been thought
again: *again-ing*, it could be said, is
intentionality personified.

There's the scene where Hulot is comforting
residual constructs: in his, always,
gestural form; that is to say: nothing
comes easy to a Christ or a Christ-like
body, once removed from its restrained
world.

You only existed, insofar, as
another recognized you, without which
you would have been voided— worthy of death.

What will you do once you've finished reading?

When Tati points to one thing instead of
something else, it is not mere discernment
(which we see all too often); herein is
a matter of sufficient importance,
wherein one either dies, is buried, or
is born again; the world of the living
contains a central distinction, namely:
between ONE and the PAIRING-FOR-LIFE-
BOUND;

simply: there are no singularities—
save for themselves, in extinction; worlds are
divided, split, discerned, paired, and DOUBLED.
Typewriters weep calmly…they are likely
not hunted as we are…moving, as we
do, with cloud and grass; the cameras weep
loudly…asking: what did I do to you?

I know the meaning of film, if only
I had the time to tell it to the one
who's reading this under a lamp shade.

THE SIXTH BOOK

Impossible Laws

THERE'S A RED STAIN
ON A WHITE NEON TUBE.

Before the play—before the act—before the light—there is the blue behind it all—voices opened on the door—feminine forms and masculine forms colliding—previous states codified in a system of shelves—what's the question we ask ourselves—transformation or metamorphosis?

(inferno)

THERE'S A GOLDEN ARROW HOVERING OVER MY HOME IN THE DESERT.

In order to be—by operatic means—in order to prepare the body—for cages, houses, and worlds— we must come to know what we're offered.

(purgatorio)

"WE."

Futurism is final and ambition remains in praxis—humiliation on the other hand, is entirely your doing—like fighting an animal until something happens.

(paradiso)

THERE'S A STAGE OF PRESENCES.

An animal sees a bird—a bird sees an animal—both are a go—this is the opera that takes us back—returning to where we came from.

CRIME & METHODOLOGY

I.

An overcoat can, essentially, be untouched—that Hebraic aside is to say: under the world, there's only fear—every estranged fact, yet to be established—cinema, at least, gives us a chance—cuts from the window—dominates the beginning, so that we might fall again—if only to split the one.

II.

A mission—wherein I might be violently contained—a red box unfolding—and what laughing might do as it turns to the monstrosity of faces—as there is always a clarity in the return—godly expectations contorting and discomforting—so much thunder—so many idiotic thresholds—to surpass.

The Double Crime

THE FLOATING PIECES—
GNOSTICALLY KNOWN
AND INSCRIBED—AFFIX
THE FABRIC TO A DENSE
TEXTURE, EMERGING—AS
IF BY DIVINE MADNESS—
FROM A RELINQUISHING
SCREAM WHICH SPILLS OUT
FROM INSIDE A LIGHTED
HOLE AND FALLS TO SEE
THE LIGHT FROM BELOW.

I WAS BORN IN AN EGG,
SOMEWHERE BETWEEN A
DESERT HOME AND THE
INTENTIONAL MESS OF
A CITY. LIGHTS FLICKERED
THERE TO REMIND US OF
STREET WORK, WHITE
NOISE, MUSIC, AND THE
KAFKAN BELITTLED ARM.

PICTURE A TORN PHOTO
IN YOUR PULSATING MIND:
THIS IS THE BEARABLE
LIGHTNESS OF BEING.

WALKING INTO A THRESHOLD-FOG IS NOT SOMETHING YOU OFTEN CATCH YOURSELF DOING BUT THE PATERNAL ANIMAL INSIDE IS ANGRY AND DOMINERRING. ONCE THE FORM IS PLACED DOWN, IT NEARLY EXPLODES. TIME DISTORTS. THE MACHINE OF EXISTENCES LEAKS OUT A BLACK LIQUID, ALMOST SEXUALLY STYLED. ALL AFFECT IS THIS—LIKE FLOWER WALLPAPER.

THE MATRON EROTICALLY
INTRUDES—THE   CHILD
BLUSHES.

AFTER EATING AN ERRATIC STAR: THE MASCULINE COUPLES, IN ORDER TO DISCOVER ANOTHER WORLD WITH NO LIGHT. THE DARK STAGE HIDES THE DARK SELF. TOUCHING, CRYING, AND ABUSING ARE MELODRAMATICALLY RENDERED ESCPAES FROM SLEEP AND FROM THE TOWERING WIND OF THE FEMININE.

SOMETHING HORRIBLE
IS ABOUT TO HAPPEN.
THE CONVALESCENCE'S
SICKNESS IS TRAPPED
IN THE CUPBOARD.
YOU INSTINCTUALLY
SYSTEMATIZE YOUR PLACE
BUT IT WON'T STOP THE
BOILING OVER.

THE STAGE IS ALL SET
FOR THE REAL MOTHER
TO APPEAR. SHE SLOW
DANCES HER WAY ONTO
IT—LIKE A CHARACTER
SHATTERING GLASS WITH
HER NECK.

DO YOU FEEL TRAPPED
IN A BLANKET WITH A
DISGUSTING   OTHER,
ANARCHICALLY MOTILE? A
GLASS OF MILK SOMETIMES
HELPS.   WHISTLING   ON
STAGE SOMETIMES HELPS.

FROM OUT OF THE DARK, A SPIDER CRAWLS OVER THE BODY OF YOUR SPOUSE. WHAT INFLUENCE IT HAS, AS YOUR SPOUSE DISAPPEARS. A THOUSAND GLASSES OF MILK ARE CONSUMED AND STILL: NOTHING.

THE INNER CRAG LOOKS
HEAVENLY IF YOU DON'T
GET TOO CLOSE, BUT TO
MEET THE ACTUAL OTHER
MEANS AN INNOCENCE
ON YOUR PART AND
YOU KNOW AS WELL AS
ANY, THAT THE SINGULAR
SELF ONLY EXISTS AND
PERSISTS BY THE ACT OF A
DEMIURGE REAPPEARING.
DID YOU NOTICE THAT
YOUR HEAD JUST FELL OFF?
YOU WERE SCREAMING AS
IT DROPPED— UNLESS, OF
COURSE, THIS IS A DREAM.

WHEN YOU PICK UP YOUR
HEAD AND PLACE IT IN THE
CHANGING   MACHINE,
CERTAIN BAD MEMORIES
ARE STOLEN AND HASTILY
GIVEN   OVER   TO   A
NOMADIC TRIBE.

I WOKE UP TO A BEATING IN THE STREET. THE IMMEDIATE ALTERITY HAD ALREADY ABANDONED ME. MY OBSESSIONAL LAUGHTER WAS A KIND OF MINOR MURDER. THE CHILD SEES THE DOOR CLOSING. CREATION WAS MOST CERTAINLY A MISTAKE.

THE DECISION TO HURT SOMETHING SMALL IS A FIRST CUT IN A DESIGN THAT DOES NOT GO ACCORDING TO PLAN. THE WOUND OPENS AND CATASTROPHE FLOODS IN. THIS IS A MAMMOTH EVENT.

THE TRANSCENDENTAL
BELIEF HAPPENS IN A
HERACLITIAN FIRE BUT
NOWHERE ELSE CAN ITS
SPHERICAL SHAPE LIVE ON.
THE DEMIURGE DIES TO
GIVE LIFE. IT EMBRACES THE
ACTUAL. IT PURIFIES.

THE LAST BOOK

Against Heidegger / Heidegger Against

Firstly, the figurative and nine knives over a red field with one blade plunged in and gray steam releasing into air—all seen in eroded strikes and the new collapsing glass from above.

Below the red field, shards raining downward into head and hand, both bleeding upwardly as if up-side-down and colliding with both glass and blood movements—the line, a segmented yellow, following the most virile path from one to the other and backward to a black ground that delimits the scene entire.

On the black liquid ground, dense and viscous, held in by thick, yet shattering glass: I stood, screaming out the selfsame black liquid in vomitous clouds roundly expanding outward until spherically perfect—these bubbles interrupt the shapes, the lines, the movements, the bodies, and freeze the scene with an absolute regulation, until only a single sphere has filled the plane with itself.

The glass has been miraculously mended
and what else there was is now as if not,
including myself which has been placed out
of the plane as mere observer—the bubble
idly waiting like a lone god.

The sphere, in almost imperceptible inflation, begins to distort to the point of implosion, and then implosion itself liquidized and poured through almost imperceptible holes in the glass, back into its containment—the center emptied out and the body, nude, placed there hovering between two glass fronted liquid black pillars.

The glass holes permanently close themselves as the body goes rigid and increasingly blushed with what looks like a dangerously applied coat of blood red paint, suffocating the breath and the capability to breathe— the body rigidly spasmodic like a jumping red arrow only pointing everlastingly away from itself to the redemptive demarcations of boundary or wall.

The red arrowed body is shot against the exterior plane, to no avail, but the visible and slowly purpling and blackening of surfaces are readily appearing as the discolored arrow is shot anterior and evermore bruised—the body beginning to drop its now pink sanguinity which loudly splats on floorward glass with deafening and blinding echo.

From the black plane a pink line quietly rises—a new body with newly ascending flesh and unknowable discernments.

The rising pink consumes the field entire with no room for the interior observer, who has been hurled beyond the wall and waits pressed against it—eyes burning in silver skull.

The figurative sable body with gleaming chromatic silver skull atop, eyes now emptied of flame, drifting from the wall, the plane, the scene entire—drifting to another uncertain diagram with all ambiguity intact and the old disappearing into the darkest of matter.

I just minced my last words with you. I am not mincing one more word with you. I am giving you your last w a r n i n g . Did you hear me give you your

last warning?
Because that was
it—what you just
heard me
utter to you,
I hope you
paid attention to
it because it was
your last warning.

Gordon Lish

The section, *The Little Legacies*, appeared in chapbook form from Glow Worm Press.

And various poems appeared in *Prelude, Dream Pop Press, Fuzz 3, and Inknode.*

Recognitions of The Absolute

Family & Friends: the few, the many.

Again, Gillian Olivia Blythe Hamel & Rusty Morrison, for duties unto care, editorship, and a home.

Iain Thomson, Elizabeth Robinson, and Brian Evenson for endorsements and my unmitigated admiration.

Santa Fe, Berkeley, Oakland, London, Sicily, and Bay Ridge most of all.

In all ways for The Reader.

And the enemies!

LM Rivera is a writer. He co-founded Called
Back Books w/ his fiancé Sharon Zetter. His
work has appeared in various small presses
and magazines. His chapbook, *The Little
Legacies*, is available from Glo Worm Press
and his first full-length book, *The Drunkards*,
is out from Omnidawn.

Against Heidegger
LM Rivera

Text set in Futura Std & Plain Germanica

Cover & Interior Design by
Sharon Zetter & Gillian Olivia Blythe Hamel
with assistance from LM Rivera
Background Cover Image: Camille Couvet
Cover photo: Carl Curmans

Printed in the United States
by Books International, Dulles, Virginia
On 50# Glatfelter B19 Antique
Acid Free Archival Quality Recycled Paper

Publication of this book was made possible in part by gifts from
Katherine & John Gravendyk in honor of Hillary Gravendyk,
Francesca Bell, Mary Mackey, and The New Place Fund

Omnidawn Publishing
Oakland, California
Staff and Volunteers, Spring 2020

Rusty Morrison & Ken Keegan, senior editors & co-publishers
Kayla Ellenbecker, production editor
Gillian Olivia Blythe Hamel, senior editor & book designer
Trisha Peck, senior editor & book designer
Rob Hendricks, marketing assistant & *Omniverse* editor
Cassandra Smith, poetry editor & book designer
Sharon Zetter, poetry editor & book designer
Liza Flum, poetry editor
Matthew Bowie, poetry editor
Juliana Paslay, fiction editor
Gail Aronson, fiction editor
Izabella Santana, fiction editor & marketing assistant
SD Sumner, copyeditor

Glamorous Deaths of the Book